Boeing 737-200
InCamera

Scott Henderson

SCOVAL
PUBLISHING LTD

© 1998 Scott Henderson
Written by Scott Henderson

**British Library Cataloguing
in Publication Data**
A catalogue record for this book is available
from the British Library

ISBN: 1 902236 00 9

Published by:
SCOVAL Publishing Ltd
PO BOX 36
Ponteland
Newcastle-upon-Tyne
NE20 9WE
Tel: (01661) 820 838
Fax: (01661) 822 911

Printed by:
Colorworks (Print Ltd), Chesterfield

Designed and typeset in 11.5pt on 13pt Lydian
by J.R. Taylor for SCOVAL Publishing Ltd

Back Cover

*Two shots of 737s in British Airways
controversial new colours, G-BGDA and G-BGDI
both taken at Manchester in October 1997.*
George Ditchfield

Acknowledgements

Special thanks to George Ditchfield and
Peter Keating from whose collection,
most of the photos in this book have been
supplied. Where known, credit has been given
but in certain instances, where the
photographer was not known, please forgive
me if due credit is not awarded.

Cover Picture

*Originally ordered by, but not delivered to,
Pacific Air Lines, this 737-293 passed through a
number of operators including Wein Consolidated
Airlines, Air California and Air Cal. Air Cal
merged with American Airlines in 1987 bringing
N461GB into the fleet. To look at this shot taken
in July 1988, its hard to believe that this
immaculate aircraft is twenty years old and only
has three years to serve before being retired to
Phoenix Arizona*

Bob Shane

The InCamera Series

This is the first in an exciting range of books which sets out to portray both Civil and Military Aircraft, both from the early days of Aviation to the present day. It covers what you (the aircraft enthusiast) have said you require, no demand — the highest standards of reproduction of some of the most beautiful photographs ever taken of Aircraft, in black and white or full colour, and wherever possible in large plate reproduction.

Whether you are an avid modeller, connected with aviation, or just interested in the beauty and mystique of aircraft, this new series of books in the range 'INCAMERA' will bring to you breathtaking images of Aircraft reproduced to the highest standards possible today. They are produced by a publisher who has in-depth knowledge of the subject as well as a vast archive which enables him to achieve the above goals. I hope that you get as much enjoyment reading this series as I did creating it.

Scott Henderson

The Boeing 737-200 InCamera

The Boeing 737 series is currently the world's best selling jet airliner, which is surprising considering the late-start made in the short-haul jet market by this, the smallest member of the Boeing family. The decision to proceed with production was announced in February 1965 on the strength of a launch order by Lufthansa for twenty-one series 100 aircraft. At the time, what seemed like its biggest rival — the British Aircraft Corporation BAC 1-11 — was in flight test with only a matter of two months to service entry with British United Airlines. The other main competitor — the Douglas DC 9 — would be taking it's first flight within three months, entering service with Delta Airlines in December 1965.

In retrospect, what seemed to be a major risk at such a late stage in the development of short-range jet aircraft for Boeing turned out to be, only a few years later, a tremendous success. For, unlike the design of the competing aircraft, both were T-Tailed and rear engine types with five abreast seating. Boeing had decided to continue with its winning formula of a wider fuselage seating six abreast, with seats, doors, ceiling, and interior panels and structural commonality with it's previous jet aircraft, the 707 and the 727. It has engines in pods under the wings, close to the fuselage of the same type as the 727, giving airlines operating a range of Boeing aircraft in their fleets a distinct advantage over the competition.

The one disadvantage of the engine location on the 737, is that the interior noise levels are somewhat higher than that of the rear engine designs, although when airline marketing departments stopped promoting one aircraft type over another and wing mounted engines became the norm in aircraft design, this problem has reduced in importance.

United Airlines ordered forty of the larger series 200 on the fifth of April 1965 .In this version, the fuselage was lengthened by six feet (1.83 metres) to provide two extra rows of seats. With a little adjustment to the interior layout this total was increased to 119, in later years, the total was increased even further to a high-density layout of an unbelievable 130 places. Used almost exclusively in the northern Countries of Europe to the Sunny Mediterranean, the 737 has served in much larger numbers than the competition, due to the fact that it could carry an average of eleven more passengers per flight, so making a considerable difference in profit to the operating airlines.When production ended in August 1988, a total of 1,144 aircraft had been delivered, comprising 30 series 100 ,249 series 200 and 865 series 200-Advanced.

First delivered to United Airlines in December 1968 and bought by Piedmont in September 1972 and named "Manhattan Pacemaker". Judging by the filthy condition of the aircraft its obvious that the maintenance crew had not been keeping pace with the cleaning to keep N749N in tip top condition.

George Ditchfield Collection

PIEDMONT

Top: *In a rare quiet moment in October 1988, N224US wears the newly revised Piedmont colour scheme. The registration has also been revised and is applied temporarily in sticker form.*
George Ditchfield Collection

Bottom: *After the merger with US Air, N209US is photographed in late 1989 wearing the final livery to grace the 737 in Piedmont service — note also that the aircraft no longer carries a name.*
George Ditchfield Collection

Photographed on a very cold morning at Manchester in January 1980, G-BMEC wears the colours of Air Europe. Delivered in May 1979, the aircraft had a short service with the airline before being sold to Guinness Peat Aviation in April 1985 for onward delivery to Western Airlines in the USA.

George Ditchfield

Basking in early morning sunshine, "Sambirano" a 737-2B2, was first delivered to the airline in December 1972. 5R-MFB has had a long ser-
vice career with Air Madagascar and is used on regional sectors in company with another 737 and a pair of British Aerospace 748s.

Scotpic

Photographed at Boeing Field just before delivery to EL AL in September 1982. 4X-ABN was actually purchased by the Israeli government for use by the airline free of charge — save that they had to meet the maintenance and insurance costs out of cash flow.

George Ditchfield Collection

Delivered new in December 1978 and still in service, 5H-ATC taxies out for take-off wearing the attractive colours of Air Tanzania which were based on the national flag.

Peter Keating

London Heathrow is the location of this stunning shot of Royal Brunei 737 VR-UEB, caught taking a break on delivery from Boeing.

Brian Stainer

ROYAL BRUNEI AIRLINES

Starting life in Europe flying for Maersk Air, C2-RN8 was bought by Air Nauru for use on regional services to Australia, New Zealand, and Singapore in September 1982.

Air Nauru

Delivered to Maersk Air in September 1980, OY-APR had a varied career over the years passing on lease from one operator to another, flying from October 1980, for 20 months, in the colours of Guyana Airways.

Pictured on approach at Kai Tak, Hong Kong, VR-HYK wears the stunning livery adopted on the formation of Dragonair in April 1985.

Scott Henderson

On a sunny day in November 1972, N453OW prepares for take-off wearing the classic Indian head livery of Western Airlines.

George Ditchfield Collection

Western

Departing from Las Vegas on a hot windy day in April 1985, N239WA taxies to the runway on the start of another sector.

Dean Slaybaugh Collection

Western

SOUTH AFRICAN AIRWAYS

Left: Sitting in regal company of a Balair Coronado on the ramp at Johannesburg, ZS-SBM 'Gamtoos' is pictured in South African Airways early springbok livery.
Brian Stainer

Top Right: Before being purchased by Comair in August 1993, ZS-SBR served South African Airways faithfully for thirteen years and is seen here in her later years in a modernised version of the springbok livery.
Peter Keating

Bottom Right: During a rare quiet moment at Jan Smuts in June 1983, ZS-SBO displays the revised S.A.A. livery, thirteen years after entering service.
Peter Keating

At Miami. 'Tjon Tjon', wears arguably one of the most attractive liverys ever to grace the 737, that of Surinam Airways for whom OY-APR served for eleven months on services to Paramaribo from May 1993.

One of a fleet of 22 Boeing 737's plying the air routes of Australia. VH-CZM takes a brief rest before push-back and another sector.

Authors Collection

 **Ansett**

On a warm sunny morning in June 1985, SU-BBW prepares to land at Frankfurt after another flight from Egypt.

Caught on a crisp clear evening in May 1995 at Norilsk Siberia, way above the Arctic Circle. YL-BAA of Transaero is prepared for a quick turnaround for the return to Moscow.

Scott Henderson

In July 1980, N493WC sits awaiting her next load of freight at Atlanta Georgia.

Bahamasair leased a total of four 737s in the 1980s, three via Guinness Peat and this aircraft, a 737-2V4 from Polaris Leasing. Here C6-BEH sits at Atlanta in January 1981 during a break in the delivery flight to Nassau.

George Ditchfield Collection

Braathens flew a total of sixteen 737-200s in the 1980s and early 1990s before being replaced by 737-400s and 500s. Here we see LN-SUQ taxiing to the runway deep in the Alps at Innsbruck.

George Ditchfield Collection

Caught on approach to Heathrow Airport in February 1979, PH-TVE is one of a number of 737s leased from Transavia in the late 1970s to replace, on a short term basis, the retirement of Tridents in the British Airways fleet until their own aircraft were delivered.

George Ditchfield Collection

Air Zimbabwe's vivid colours are reflected on Z-NAL in the early morning light at Harare Airport in January 1986, in the distinguished presence of a company Viscount.

On a rare sunny morning at Manchester's Ringway Airport in June 1985, EC-DVN of Spanish inclusive tour operator Hispania, makes an impressive sight on push-back, on the start of another flight of holidaymaker's to sunny Spain.

George Ditchfield

SINGAPORE AIRLINES LIMITED

Left: *Bought to replace Comets on internal and medium range routes, M.S.A. had the distinction of being the first operator of the 737 in Asia. This photograph of 9V-BBC taken at Singapore on 31st of August 1969 is taken exactly one month after entering service.*

Peter Keating

Top Right: *Photographed at Singapore on the 14th of July 1972, 9V-BFD displays the subtle change of livery on the road to the break-up of the airline in October 1972 to form Singapore Airlines and Malaysian Airlines System.*

Peter Keating

Bottom Right: *Originally delivered to M.S.A. as 9M-AOW in October 1969, 9V-BFF was re-registered on the formation of Singapore Airlines in September 1972 and in this attractive livery flew the last years of service before being sold to Air Florida in 1980.*

Peter Keating

On approach to Osaka on a midsummer's day in July 1979, JA8453 is photographed just a matter of eighteen days after delivery looking, of course, brand new.

K Murai via George Ditchfield

Serving alongside seven 200 series and fourteen 500 series 737s in the fleet of Air Nippon, JA-8455 looks as good as new even after eighteen years of service in Japan.

Authors Collection

Caught on quick turnaround in March 1980 at Colombo Sri-Lanka, 4R-ALC is a rare sight to behold to European eyes.

Peter Keating

Photographed at Nairobi, Kenya in July 1975 and displaying the rarely seen colours of DETA Mozambique. CR-BAA was first delivered in December 1969 and is one of four 737s to serve with the airline.

Peter Keating

Shot in March 1981, in the exotic livery of Thai Airways which was, at that time, the internal service carrier of Thailand. HS-TBA prepares to depart on another sector.

Under ominous skies at Bangkok in September 1988, HS-TBE sports the livery that was adopted fleet-wide after the merger between Thai Airways and Thai International in April 1988.

 **Thai**

After an early life serving in the fleet of Britannia Airways, G-BAZI was purchased in March 1985 to serve alongside two BAC 1-11's in the fleet of this small charter airline, Airways Cymru based in Cardiff, Wales. Cymru is Welsh for Wales.

George Ditchfield

航 代 國 中

B-2503

BOEING 737

TRANSCORP

The Civil Aviation Administration of China ordered ten 737s in November 1982, to start the process of replacing the Hawker Siddeley Trident. Delivered on the first of March 1983, B-2503 is seen here at Hong Kong, taxiing for take-off back to mainland China.

Arthur J Payne via George Ditchfield

Air Zaïre operated N331XV under lease from Polaris Aircraft Leasing Corporation from May 1990 to July 1991, after which the aircraft was withdrawn from service and placed in storage in Phoenix Arizona.

George Ditchfield Collection

Originally owned by Malaysia-Singapore Airlines before sale to Air Florida, YV-405C, a 737-112 was shot on delivery to Savor, of Venezuela, in February 1992. Note that Air Florida registration is displayed in the windows to the rear of the aircraft.

Authors Collection

Looking decidedly psychedelic in its "Flower Power" scheme, N73711 of Aloha Airlines taxies to the gate after another inter-island flight in September 1979. Unfortunately the aircraft was written-off in an accident at Hilo Hawaii in April 1988.

George Ditchfield Collection

Top Right: *N730AL sits on the ramp at Honolulu in the unimaginative livery carried in the late 70's and early 80's.*
George Ditchfield Collection

Bottom Right: *Looking very exotic in the latest colours, N70723 a 737-297 Advanced, basks in the sun waiting for a tug to put her back to work.*
Bob Shane

This aircraft was illustrated earlier in this book flying for Hispania as EC-DVN. Wearing Transavia livery, PH-TVS is pushed-back at Manchester under stormy skies in November 1980.

George Ditchfield

CP-Air 737 CF-CPV was shot about to roll on take-off at San Francisco in November 1971.

Dean Slaybaugh

On a crisp clear November morning in 1982, N331DL is prepared for its initial delivery to Delta Airlines.

Delivered to Lufthansa in June 1968, N408PE a 737-130 was bought by People Express in April 1981, serving with them until their merger with Continental Airlines in 1987.

George Ditchfield Collection

Purchased new in August 1988. A40-BF in its "GOLDEN FALCON" livery of Gulf Air must be one of the most attractive colour schemes flown in the last 25 years.

Authors Collection

 GULFAIR

Photographed at Prague Czechoslovakia, YI-AGH was delivered new to the airline in August 1974. Unfortunately, due to UN Sanctions, she has been grounded at Wadi-al-Therthar, Iraq since 1991 so the chances of her flying again are slim.

Manchester is the location of this Air Portugal 737, which seems to have spent its entire life on short term lease. In fact, at the time this shot was taken in November 1991, it had completed seventeen leases with eight major airlines.

George Ditchfield

Taken in December 1980 when she was barely a year old, N53AF sits on a rather grubby ramp wondering, no doubt, where she will be flying to next.

Croatia Airlines formed from the break-up of Yugoslavia, flies a total of five 737s on European routes. Here we have 9A-CTD on approach to London's Heathrow in June 1997.

Scott Henderson

Although now withdrawn from use and stored at Dublin, EI-BEB "St Eunan" spent over thirteen years flying the air routes between Ireland and the UK before being leased for a 'last fling' of service in Australia with East West Airlines.

Scott Henderson

Aer Lingus

G-AVRL

BRITANNIA AIRWAYS

BOEING 737

On a typical summer's day in August 1968 at Gatwick Airport, G-AVRL of Britannia Airways awaits passengers before flying to sunnier climes ,having the distinction of being the first 737-200 delivered to the airline and the first to enter service in Europe on 7th of July 1968.

George Ditchfield Collection

Britannia

Top: *The setting is Manchester in April 1981 and standing on the sunny ramp is G-AVRM in Britannia livery, still looking rather youthful considering delivery took place twelve years previously.*

George Ditchfield

Bottom: *Britannia Airways used G-BGYK "Reginald J Mitchell" on inclusive tour services from the UK to many Mediterranean resorts. Here seen returning to Newcastle from Malaga, Spain in the final colours worn in the last years of service with the airline.*

Scott Henderson

Air Sinai uses its single 737 SU-GAN to transport mainly tourists to over half-a-dozen domestic destinations from its base at Cairo.

George Ditchfield Collection

Photographed in June 1993 whilst under lease to Sultan Air of Turkey. TC-VAB has had a varied career serving with over eleven airlines since being delivered new to Aer Lingus in January 1970.

Delivered new to Sahsa in October 1994, HR-SHA was destined to serve the airline for close to sixteen years until being damaged beyond repair after overrunning the runway at San Jose, Costa Rica in November 1991.

George Ditchfield Collection

SAHSA
SERVICIO AEREO DE HONDURAS·S.A.

This shot, taken in May 1980 just after delivery brand-new from Boeing, displays C-GLPW in the stylish colours of Western Pacific which were carried until the merger with Canadian Airlines International in April 1987.

For a total of five years, four months CC-CIM flew in the service of Ledaco of Chile until being sold to America West in April 1986.

Malev had the distinction of being the first Soviet Client State to put a Boeing aircraft into service when three 737-200's were leased in the last months of 1988. HA-LEC was photographed at Zurich in 1989 in the stunning new scheme especially devised for the new aircraft.

George Ditchfield Collection

On a sunny day in September 1981 N464GB is caught on approach to Los Angeles in the vibrant colours of Air California.

Originally delivered new to United Airlines in October 1968, N459AC spent a good deal of time on lease to Aloha before joining the fleet of Air California in October 1980. On change of name to Air Cal in April 1981 this flamboyant livery was adopted fleetwide.

George Ditchfield Collection

AIRCAL

On a sunny day in June 1983 F-GBYH glides into another landing at Heathrow Airport.

Scott Henderson

AIR FRANCE ////

On a stormy October morning in 1991 F-GBYF sports the experimental livery that was never adopted fleet wide.

George Ditchfield

UNITED

Left: Delivered to United Airlines in October 1968, less than a year after the 737 was first certified, "City of Medford" wears the Stars and Bars Friend Ship colours on a wet and chilly morning in 1970.

Scotpic

Top Right: First delivered to Frontier Airlines in November 1978 as N7398F and then purchased by United Airlines in June 1985 and re-registered in June 1986. N984UA was photographed in July 1989 in United's attractive "Double U" livery.

Tim William's

Bottom Right: Photographed in May 1996, in that notoriously difficult scheme to shoot, N9032U looks brand-new after nearly 27 years of service for United Airlines.

Authors Collection

Delivered new to Maersk in January 1979, OY-APK displays the stunning blue livery of this Danish Airline in this shot taken in May 1980.

George Ditchfield Collection

Photographed in September 1981 being prepared for delivery to Tame, the Domestic Airline of Ecuador, "Ciudad De Loja" was destined to be the sole 737-200 to serve with the airline. She met an unfortunate end on 11th of July 1983 when, after a brief sixteen months of service, she crashed while landing at Cuenta, Ecuador.

Dean Slaybaugh

Bought new in May 1980, C-GQBB wears the regal livery of Quebecair on a cold clear morning in January 1981.

Gary Vincent via George Ditchfield

Acquired upon the merger with People Express in February 1987, N402PE a 737-130 proudly displays the striking classic Continental colours in February 1990.

George Ditchfield Collection

Bought from Air Algeria in June 1982, TZ-ADL served alongside a sole 727-100 in the colours of Air Mali for three years, five months before onward sale to United Aviation Services.

Michel Gilland via George Ditchfield Collection

Purchased from Midway Airlines in May 1991, V5-ANA still serves as the sole 737 in the now renamed Air Namibia's fleet, on services in the African Continent radiating from Windhoek.

Peter Keating

Under lease from Guinness Peat Aviation in November 1983 EC-DTR served with this Spanish Inclusive Tour Airline alongside a fleet of Convairs classic 990 Coronados until return in February 1988 just before the collapse of the Airline.

Scotpic

Photographed landing at Zurich in July 1983 OO-SDB was delivered new to the airline in May 1974 and used by Sabena until February 1988.

Scotpic

Slowly taxiing at Manchester in September 1993, OO-SDG sports the latest colours of Sabena the Belgian State Airline.

George Ditchfield

Wearing the definitive 70s colour scheme, brown and ochre, C-FTAN is seen taxiing at Toronto in June 1978 complete with stone deflectors on the nosewheel. Delivered in April 1970, the aircraft remained in the fleet until Transair merged with Pacific Western in 1979.

Authors Collection

Caught on approach to Heathrow Airport in June 1980, D-ABEB was the third 737-130 manufactured by Boeing and was delivered to Lufthansa in December 1967. Although nearly fourteen years old at the time this shot was taken on the 11th of June 1980, the aircraft was still in immaculate condition.

Peter Keating

Top Right: "Ah" what might have been. D-ABFW "Wolfberg" taxies-by in August 1988 in the experimental colours that, unfortunately, were not adopted by Lufthansa.

Christofer Witt via George Ditchfield Collection

Bottom Right: On lease to Lufthansa from Condor for five months in 1982-83, D-ABHD displays an interesting livery! Sadly, after return to Condor, the aircraft was lost when it crashed on approach to Izmir, Turkey on the 2nd of January 1988.

George Ditchfield Collection

Just about number one in the list of unusual airline liveries must be Casino Express of Elko Nevada. who use, the two 737s which form the fleet to transport holidaymakers from across the USA to the gambling casinos of its home town in real style.

Bob Shane

Photographed at Athens in March 1993 SX-BCA "Apollo" is captured in the multi-coloured livery of Olympic Airways.

OLYMPIC

Formed in 1992, Ukraine International's total fleet consists of two 737s. Here photographed on a hot day in August 1996, UR-GAC taxiies to the runway at Malaga, southern Spain for a return flight to Kiev.

Scott Henderson

Looking brand-new whilst on delivery to Airfast of Indonesia in September 1991. It is hard to believe that PK-OCG was first registered twenty years earlier to Air California in May 1971.

Bob Shane

Following arrival at Lusaka in April 1988, 9J-AEG is shown in Zambia Airways flamboyant colours.

  Zambia Airways

Pictured at Jorge Newbury Aeroparque in Buenos Aires in June 1995, LV-JTO was celebrating 25 years in service and doesn't she look good!

AEROLINEAS ARGENTINAS

Acquired on the merger with Air Cal in July 1987, N461GB served a total of four years, three months before being withdrawn from use.

Bob Shane via George Ditchfield Collection

Caught two months after delivery at Manchester in May 1980, the new G-BGTV is pushed back in preparation for another flight to Spain. Notice the smoky departure of a BAC-1-11 in the background.

George Ditchfield

A wonderful shot of PP-VMJ in the classic livery of Varig taken at Rio in July 1986. This aircraft was lost in a crash, 55 kms from San Jose Do Xingu, Brazil in September 1989.

George Ditchfield Collection

  VARIG

Royal Air Maroc, CN-RMK "Smara", captured on approach to Malaga Airport in August 1997.

royal air maroc

Delivered new in July 1980, "Pikakawaka" of Air New Zealand is photographed in September 1980 under threatening skies at Christchurch while sub-leased to Polynesian Airlines.

NAC

Top Right: *Originally delivered to New Zealand National Airways Corporation in August 1968, ZK-NAC spent a grand total of six years, nine months flying for Air New Zealand before being sold to CG Air leasing in 1986. In August 1992 the aircraft was broken up for parts recovery at Mojave California.* Scotpic

Bottom Right: *Here we see ZK-NAC in the scheme carried in her days of service with New Zealand National Airways Corporation.* Scotpic

wings of the nation

Photographed in March 1972 during a fruitless sales visit at the Qantas Base in Australia, N1359B sits in company with the more successful 707. As it turned out, Boeing would have to wait until March 1980 until the breakthrough order for the 737 was received from Ansett. This was for twelve 737-200 Advanced models which opened the floodgates for the 737 in the Australian Market.

Most famous in Europe as being a major operator of the Tupolev 134, Aviogenex of the now defunct state of Yugoslavia also operated four 737s, one of them being YU-ANP shown here at Manchester just after push-back preparing for another flight to the sunny Mediterranean in June 1989.

George Ditchfield

On lease from FSBU Corporation, N239TA displays the exotic livery of TACA Transportes Aereos de El Salvidor one of fifteen 737's in the fleet.

Author Collection

Delivered to Wein Air Alaska in June 1979, G-BKNH passed through the hands of Dan Air London between March 1983 and March 1987, before travelling south for service with Mandala Airlines of Indonesia. Here the aircraft is seen just prior to push-back at Newcastle on 24th of August 1983 on one of the regular visits to, what at that time, was a major Dan Air Hub.

DAN+AIR

Scott Henderson

Photographed during a brief stop at London's Heathrow Airport on delivery to Indian Airlines in April 1971, VT-EAM was to have a short service life with the airline before being destroyed in May 1973 after hitting power lines when coming into land at Deli-Palam Airport, India.

Brian Stainer

Shot on a rare sunny day at Newcastle in March 1990, 9H-ABB of Air Malta displays the company's stylish colours whilst on turn-around for the journey back home.

Authors Collection

Owned by Thai Airlines AP-BEW was leased by Shaheen International Airways — a small charter operator based in Karachi Pakistan — between January 1994 and April 1996. The aircraft was repossessed and stored at Bangkok — withdrawn from use.

On a sunny day in October 1991 at Manchester, SE-DLD of Time Air Sweden taxies slowly to the runway.

George Ditchfield

Sadly, the distinctive livery of Cruzeiro disappeared when it merged with Varig in January 1993 — bringing to an end 66 years of history. Here we see PP-CJO, a 737 Super Advanced, preparing to fly another sector within Brazil in June 1991.

George Ditchfield Collection

CX-BON stands awaiting passengers in February 1989, being one of three 737s in the fleet bought to replace Vickers Viscounts in the 1980s which are used on regional routes from Montevideo Uruguay.

George Ditchfield Collection

Serving under lease for a period of sixteen years from GATX Boothe, N7378F is caught on an early morning roll for take-off in December 1975.
Dean Slaybaugh

FRONTIER AIRLINES

Top Right: *Delivered new to Frontier Airlines in October 1978, N7396F was one of 25 737s flown by the carrier in this colour scheme, before being sold to United Airlines in June 1985.*

George Ditchfield Collection

Bottom Right: *Photographed in the evening on climbout from Denver International Airport in June 1997, N205AU displays the superb updated modern livery of the Frontier Airlines of today.*

Scott Henderson

Today one of the most consistently profitable airlines in the USA with a fleet consisting totally of the 737. With this aircraft N85SW, photographed in September 1982 when only three months old, we return to the days when Southwest was smaller and the colouring to the fuselage roof was of a greener shade than at present but still very attractive never the less.

George Ditchfield Collection

Delivered to Alaska Airlines in May 1981, this 737 has the distinction of being the second delivered to the airline. Here N730AS displays the latest colours in this shot taken in February 1993.

Frank Morton via George Ditchfield Collection

Canadien was one of a number of carriers that seemed to adopt a very similar colour scheme in the 1980s. Here we have a reflective shot of one of their many 737s taken in February 1988.

Scotpic

This aircraft which forms the total fleet of NICA Nicaragua, is photographed on approach to Miami Florida in August 1993 dodging the thunderstorms just like the photographer!

Scott Henderson

Now flying as an executive jet for Elta Electronics, N70724 spent a number of years flying around Europe in the 80's named "Clipper Spreeathen" in the classic Pan Am livery, caught here on approach to Frankfurt in May 1985.

Scotpic

Although broken-up in April 1994, here we see N64AF when in happier days flying the air routes of the USA in the "billboard" scheme of Pan Am in March 1988.

PAN AM

Scotpic

Left: This is one of many 737s originally owned by Britannia Airways and leased through the present owner Boeing within the Ryanair Fleet. EI-CJE arrives in Malaga with a full load of Holidaymakers in August 1997.

Scott Henderson

Top Right: Photographed in Manchester in December 1996 we see the flying Santa Clause courtesy of Ryanair.

George Ditchfield

Bottom Right: Here we have another "Logojet" scheme by Ryanair but this time the livery is 'real class' advertising the symbol of Jaguar cars.

Authors Collection

Bought to replace the long serving BAC 1-11s in the fleet , DQ-FDM makes a splendid sight as she taxies in at Nandi in December 1987.

George Ditchfield Collection

Owned by the little-known carrier Arabia of Egypt for eleven months in 1981, SU-BCJ was sold on to Guinness Peat Aviation to continue a life of wandering between different carriers before being leased to LACSA in 1985 to join the six 737s already in the fleet.

George Ditchfield Collection

Yet another aircraft that has met an unfortunate end is B-180 of China Airlines Taiwan pictured here, which crashed on take off at Hualien, Taiwan on the 26th of October 1989.

George Ditchfield Collection

One of a number of 737-200s used by the German charter carrier Hapag-Lloyd in the 80s and early 90s to ferry holidaymakers to Mediterranean Resorts.

Christopher Witt via George Ditchfield Collection

113

Bought from South African Airways in July 1993, LV-WBO of Lineas Aereas Privadas Argentinas SA, makes an impressive sight arriving at Jorge Newbury Aeroparque, Argentina in June 1995.

Owned from new by the GATX Leasing Corporation, XA-SLC joined the fleet of TAESA, Transportes Aereos Ejecutivos SA, a small Mexican domestic airline for nineteen months from November 1993.

Dirk Spalding

Entering the fleet of Lithuanian Airlines in June 1995, to join two sister 737s and eleven Yak 42s in the service of this former Soviet carrier, LY-BSD was photographed on a pleasant sunny morning at Amsterdam Schipol in July 1995.

Scott Henderson

AIR ALGÉRIE

Top Right: One of fifteen 737s in the fleet, 7T-VEF glides into a landing on a bright sunny morning at Paris Orly in January 1982.

George Ditchfield Collection

Bottom Right: Tunis Air 737 TS-IOE is taxiing for take-off from Manchester in June 1989. The aircraft was first delivered to the airline in April 1981 and is still in-service.

George Ditchfield

With thrust reversers still in operation, TF-VLT of Eagle Air of Iceland grinds to a halt at Zurich Switzerland on the 10th of June 1984.

Werner Aegerter

Now flying with Aerosweet Airlines of the Ukraine, 9M-MBZ was photographed at Kuala Lumpur in 1987 when in-service with Malaysian Airlines System.

Peter Keating

 mas
malaysian airline system

Japan Transocean Air has fourteen 737s in its fleet that are painted in this rather stylish livery which, of course, is very similar to the parent company Japan Airlines.

Y Kurimoto via George Ditchfield Collection